REAL WORLD ECONOMICS™

How the
Gold Standard
Works

Peter Ryan

ROSEN
PUBLISHING®

New York

Published in 2011 by The Rosen Publishing Group, Inc.
29 East 21st Street, New York, NY 10010

Library of Congress Cataloging-in-Publication Data

Ryan, Peter K.
How the gold standard works / Peter K. Ryan.—1st ed.
    p. cm.—(Real world economics)
Includes bibliographical references and index.
ISBN 978-1-4488-1272-1 (library binding)
1. Gold standard—Juvenile literature. I. Title.
HG297R93 2011
332.4'222—dc22

                                                    2010012565

Manufactured in the United States of America

CPSIA Compliance Information: Batch #W11YA: For further information, contact Rosen Publishing, New York, New York, at 1-800-237-9932.

On the cover: Bars of gold are stored in the gold vault at the Federal Reserve Bank in New York.

Contents

INTRODUCTION

We all know what we can buy with $1, perhaps a soda or a candy bar. We know what things cost, but do we know what $1 is worth? Today in the United States and in most countries around the world, money's value is determined by trade between individuals, businesses, banks, and governments. Each currency has a value that is determined by the complex and mostly invisible world of trade and finance that surrounds us all the time. Our money really is just a whole lot of paper and numbers, but it is backed by the good faith of our government.

Until 1971, the U.S. dollar was also valued in gold. Each dollar in the hands of the public was worth an actual amount of gold. Anyone could go and trade his or her paper dollars for gold. This monetary system was called the gold standard and it was used all over the world.

Gold has always been a very important part of our financial system. Its properties made it a great tool for managing

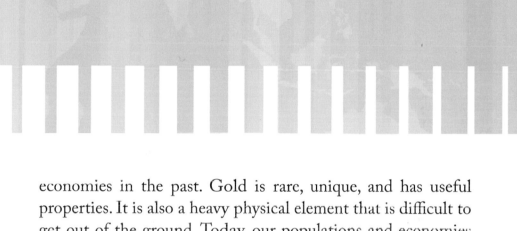

economies in the past. Gold is rare, unique, and has useful properties. It is also a heavy physical element that is difficult to get out of the ground. Today, our populations and economies have grown too large for gold to be a practical form of money. Imagine how much gold would have to be moved between banks to keep up with the pace of today's economy.

In the United States, we value our money by the good faith and continued well-being of our government. Dollars can no longer be traded for gold at the Federal Reserve. Instead, the U.S. dollar is based on a fiat currency system ("fiat," from Latin, means "let it be done"). This means each dollar is backed by faith in the entire system and the economy around it. In this book, you will learn about the gold standard and fiat currency to better understand how money works and where our monetary system is headed.

Throughout the discussion of gold, supply and demand are often mentioned and are necessary to fully understand how the

Each gold bullion bar weighs more than 27 pounds (12.2 kilograms). These bars are moved between countries in order for governments to function and do business with each other.

gold standard works. In fact, understanding supply and demand is important to understanding most economic concepts.

"Supply" refers to the availability of goods, services, or money provided to an economy by any person, group or circumstance.

6

Gold supply, for example, is the amount of gold that is available for purchase in the gold market. The supply of gold comes from the people who extract gold from the ground and from people who currently own gold and wish to sell it.

"Demand" refers to the intent to purchase or consume a product, service, or currency. Gold demand, for example, is the total amount of gold that is sought for purchase by all of the people in the gold market. People demand gold for many reasons, ranging from jewelry manufacturing and dentistry, to electronics production and investing.

The importance of studying and understanding the gold standard is made plainly evident by current events. Since 2008, the U.S. economy has been in recession, jobs have been lost, and financial value has eroded. In two short years, we have been through the worst financial crisis since the Great Depression. And as of this writing, the end is not yet in sight.

In addition to the United States, many other countries have faced very serious financial problems as well. European,

Asian, Indian, Pacific, South American, and Arabian nations have all been greatly impacted by the troubles that began in the United States. Most recently, Greece has been found to be in serious financial jeopardy. The reasons behind these troubles are complex and numerous, but by understanding how our global currency systems operated in the past, we may be able to get a better understanding of why we are in this situation today.

As a result of the financial troubles that we face today, there has been a renewed call for the resumption of the gold standard system. There is no way to know if we will go back to a gold standard. Hopefully, we'll better understand why some experts feel that the gold standard can be our way out of these troubling times.

CHAPTER ONE

THE GOLD STANDARD: AN INTRODUCTION

In order to understand both the gold standard and the fiat currency system, we first need to consider what makes up an economy and how money works in that economy. An economy is a system of making and buying goods (such as food and cell phones) and services (like getting a haircut). In this book, the economy can refer to either the world economy or the U.S. economy.

Production involves making items from start to finish. This includes taking raw materials (such as oil) out of the earth, making a product from these raw materials, and then distributing the products to stores so that people can buy them. Throughout the production process, many people are involved and all of them are paid for their labor, or work. The cost of the labor is added to the price of the product, which is then passed on to the consumer, and the production cycle continues. Consumption is the purchase of these products by consumers. The consumer wants and is able to exchange his or her money for a good or service.

Derricks pump away day and night around the world to extract oil, the precious commodity we use to drive our cars, heat our homes, and create electricity.

The producer and the consumer are involved in a transaction, or the exchange of a product for money. The producer receives payment and uses this money to make more products. The consumer receives the product in exchange for his or her

money. This system depends on trust and a shared value of the money being used.

In addition to people buying and selling in countries like the United States, people trade goods between countries. Companies in the United States purchase goods from countries like China all the time. Different countries have different currencies. For example, the United States uses the U.S. dollar, and China use a currency called the yuan. In the past, governments kept a gold reserve and actually moved the gold between countries when the cash moved around. Today, our money moves freely based on the supply of and demand for our currency.

During the time of the gold standard, each country held a balance of gold in its national treasury. Governments were required to maintain enough gold in their reserves in order to convert all of their paper money into gold. To keep up with a growing economy, governments would buy gold from other countries to match the amount of paper money in the economy. The same was also true for countries with a shrinking

11

economy. A government would sell gold to other countries to reflect less money in the economy. This would also help maintain the value of gold.

The Gold Standard in Everyday Life

Let's think about money on a personal level. Imagine that you have a job, such as selling lemonade. You have to buy all of the ingredients to make the lemonade and then sell it to customers willing to pay for it. Sometimes, you may have a customer whom you know and trust ask if he or she can have a glass of lemonade now, with a promise to pay later. Because you know and trust this person, you agree. Now, imagine that a stranger walks by and asks if he or she can have a glass of lemonade and pay you later, too. You don't know or trust this person, so you aren't certain that you will get the money later as promised. What do you do?

This example helps you understand how transactions are conducted. First, there is an exchange between the buyer and the seller. This can be cash, or it can be a promise. The cash is safe because you can use it immediately to purchase goods and services. A promise may be as safe as cash, but it can't be spent until the cash is acquired from the person who made the promise.

Throughout history, people have used coins and rare metals to conduct trade. Gold, silver, and gems were the most commonly recognized coins of trade in Western civilizations. People would develop regional trade currency standards and stick to them in order to create a system that was more easily understood by everyone. For example, when European

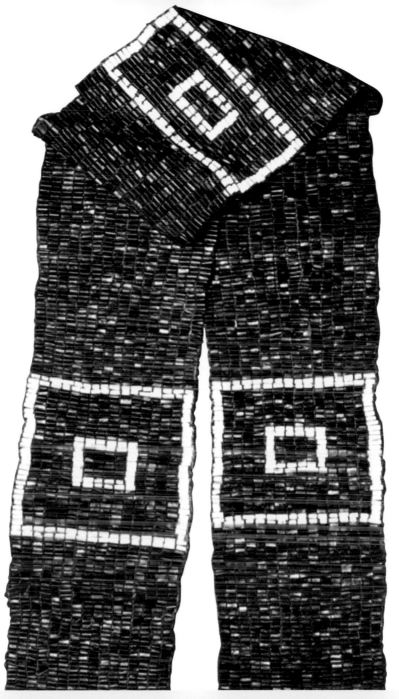

Wampum were purple shells that would be woven into belts, such as this one made by the Iroquois, and used as currency for trade. Wampum was recognized as a valid currency in many Native American nations.

settlers first landed on the shores of America, they brought gold and silver with them to trade with. They met many Indian tribes who used wampum to trade with among themselves. Wampum is a kind of shell that was often strung on belts or sashes. When the Europeans attempted trade with the Indians, their coins meant nothing to the Indians, and the Indians' wampum meant nothing to the settlers. This was because there was no way to account for the value of one gold coin or one piece of wampum. So instead, the Indians and the settlers used a pure barter system to conduct trade. Bartering is a system of trade in which people exchange physical goods directly and do not use money at all. Indians and settlers traded food, clothing, and technology with each other, allowing both sides to get something of value out of each trade.

Although the barter system is easy to understand and is efficient, there are times when bartering becomes difficult. For instance, how would you manage to trade eggs for a car? Sometimes, it is also hard for a buyer and a seller to decide on a fair price. Just how many eggs is a car worth? And finally, some goods (such as eggs) are perishable (spoil quickly) or hard to carry, which can make bartering even more challenging.

But money changed all of this. It has a stated value and is easy to carry. Currency is also a practical way of carrying out transactions of large value. For example, each time you earn a paycheck, you receive a payment that can be deposited in your bank account. Under a gold standard system, you would actually be able to take your paycheck to the bank, deposit it, and take out an amount of gold equaling the total dollars in your paycheck.

The United States and the Bimetallic Standard

Although historians commonly refer to the U.S. currency system as having been a gold standard system, it was actually a bimetallic system. In the United States, both gold and silver were the basis of the dollar. This allowed people to redeem cash for silver, cash for gold, and silver for gold. It also allowed countries to have more flexibility in changing the amount of money in the economy (also known as monetary policy).

Paper money was commonly used to conduct the majority of business. Each paper dollar was worth some amount of silver or gold, or a combination of both. People could redeem their paper money for both gold and silver.

The reason for the double system was the power and influence of the silver industry in the United States for many decades. The silver industry spent lots of time and money to convince government officials of the importance and value of silver. Politicians felt it was good to have a bimetallic system because the United States was so naturally rich with silver deposits, and mining for silver created jobs and economic growth.

GOLD RESERVES

Since we already know that people perform labor (or work), purchase (or buy) goods and services, and use money, we can examine the gold standard. The gold standard is a means of creating a ground floor upon which trade and currency can be built. By using gold as the basis for trade, it was easier to establish price standards and exchange standards.

15

The Great Depression forced nearly a quarter of the U.S. population into unemployment. Food pantries and food lines were the primary sources of food for many Americans.

This was very important because during the peak of the gold standard era, communication was not as fast as it is today. Prices of goods and services were not equal in many places, and oftentimes there weren't standard currencies that could be widely

accepted as forms of payment. So gold was the best way to determine the value of trade.

The use of gold helped the economy grow and the cost of goods increase at a steady pace. But with these benefits came downsides. First, gold frequently needed to be transported, creating lots of opportunities for theft. Second, moving gold is very expensive, requiring banks and couriers to spend lots of money to keep the gold safe and physically move it around. Finally, gold was a limited resource. Even when it was being pulled out of the ground as fast as possible, there still wasn't enough to keep up with the growth of the economy.

During World War I, the Great Depression, and World War II, so many people tried to redeem their paper money for gold that the banks ran out. The banks tried to get gold from the Federal Reserve (the U.S. central bank), but they still could not get it fast enough to keep up with the demand. So in each of these periods, the U.S. government temporarily cancelled the right to exchange money for gold. During World War II, people even had to surrender their gold to the government to help with the war effort. After each period, the government reinstated the gold standard and restored the redemption rights of the people to get gold for their money.

One of the lasting impacts of the forced redemption of gold by U.S. citizens to the government was the cultural phenomenon of gold hoarding. People came to believe that at any time they could be forced to give their gold to the government, so they began to save it. The idea of family gold became very important to many who had lived through the crushing unemployment of the Great Depression. These were the early seeds of the dissenting minority who to this day still believe that the gold standard is the only truly just and self-corrective monetary system. The divide between the gold standard advocates and the modern economists has remained constant.

CHAPTER TWO
UNDERSTANDING THE GOLD STANDARD

Now that we understand the idea behind using the gold standard, we need to learn more about how it works. Economists generally claim that there were three distinct gold standards used in the nineteenth and twentieth centuries: the gold specie standard, the gold exchange standard, and the gold bullion standard.

The gold specie standard involved people using actual gold coins to buy goods and services. This meant that a lot of gold changed hands every day.

The gold exchange standard is a system in which people used a paper currency or other forms of money, but the currency was exchangeable for a set amount of gold. This is an example of a fixed rate. A country would fix the value of its currency to a certain amount of gold. The gold exchange standard also applied to the exchange of currencies between nations. A country could figure out how much its currency was worth compared to other countries that also fixed their currencies' values in gold.

The gold bullion standard evolved last and is a system in which central governments trade gold bullion with other nations at a globally standard price and settle the international balance of accounts and the government spending. In this system, citizens were not allowed to convert their cash into gold, but an important part of the value of their money was based on the balance of gold reserves held by their country.

Central Banking

As the gold standard evolved over time, the government became a more important part of the process. In the gold specie standard, gold was freely traded for goods and services anywhere at anytime. In the gold bullion standard, gold was not used by the average citizen. This is part of the evolution away from using gold as a standard of exchange and toward using another form of currency.

This transformation was possible because of the growing importance of institutions called central banks. Every country has a central bank. A central bank is different from a regular bank: the average person cannot go to a central bank and deposit a paycheck. There are no checking accounts or savings accounts. A central bank only lends to and borrows money from other banks and governments. A central bank is, in other words, the bank for banks.

U.S. Federal Reserve Chairman Ben Bernanke testifies before a Senate Banking and Finance Committee during the financial crisis of 2008.

When the gold standard existed, it was the central bank that could affect the rate of inflation by adding or removing currency from the hands of the public. Inflation is a rise in the general prices of commonly used goods and services, such as houses, cars, and gas. Under the gold standard, that meant adding or removing gold from the hands of the commercial banks to slow or speed the rate of lending that took place. This also affected the cost of borrowing money, known as the interest rate. Today, central banks still affect the amount and cost of borrowing money, but they no longer do it by changing the amount of gold available in the economy.

In the United States, the central bank is called the Federal Reserve. In 1913, this central bank was created by a law called the Federal Reserve Act. The U.S. Federal Reserve is the single largest holder of gold in the world today, with about $140 billion in gold in its main vault in New York City.

Economics, Trade, and Commerce

The Federal Reserve is independent from the U.S. government, so it can make decisions about the U.S. economy based on rational economic principles and without any political pressures. This political independence is important for the health of the U.S. economy and all of its trading partners around the world. The Federal Reserve's role is to monitor the performance of the economy and use its tools to speed up or slow down the growth of the money supply, or the amount of money available in the economy. Under the gold standard, the money supply grew at a stable rate of 3 percent to 5 percent per year because of the physical constraints of gold extraction and management.

Where Gold Comes From

Gold is a metal we extract from the earth through mining. The primary places on Earth where gold is very abundant and extracted in large quantities are South Africa followed by the United States and then Australia. Gold mining is very difficult, dangerous, and costly. There are many methods for extracting gold, including blasting with dynamite, panning water sources, and chemical process extraction.

When gold comes out of the ground, it is typically not very large nor very pure. Most often, gold is extracted as small nuggets attached to rocks and minerals. These small nuggets are melted under high temperatures to separate the gold metal from the other minerals and metals that are not desired.

Once the gold has been isolated and melted down to more pure levels, it is stored in gold vaults for protection. The gold is sold throughout the world through the various gold trading markets, where buyers and sellers come together to agree upon a price for the transaction.

Because gold is so valuable, it is a very likely target for theft. So it has to be carefully guarded at all times. In addition to gold being very valuable, it is also very difficult to move around. So it requires lots of manpower and machinery to manage and move. It is for this reason that central governments are typically the primary holders of gold reserves.

The Federal Reserve had to keep enough gold in its vaults to pay back a certain percentage of all U.S. dollars. In theory, the Federal Reserve should have had enough gold to deliver 100 percent of the U.S. currency, but that wasn't possible because not all of the gold in the economy was in the hands of the Federal Reserve. Therefore, the Federal Reserve, using intensive study, had to estimate what amount of gold it must have in reserve to be prepared for a worst-case scenario.

This may sound scary, but the U.S. economy has experienced such situations: since the beginning of the twentieth century, there have been several times when so many people demanded their gold that the Federal Reserve had to temporarily suspend the gold reserve or risk depleting the entire gold reserve of the United States.

CURRENCY

There were three different gold standards, and the oldest was the gold specie standard. This system began in the earliest days of civilization, dating back to the early Byzantine Empire.

Valuable gold coins were exchanged in transactions as simple as buying bread and as important as funding wars. A coin's value was determined by its weight and nothing more. Because metallurgy (the study of metals) was still a very new science, it was

This bronze coin from the Ostrogoth Empire would have been minted between 534 and 536 CE. Bronze was used because of the abundance of the material in that region.

nearly impossible to determine the purity of gold or any other rare metal or precious stone. Basic weights and measurements were used. To help simplify the exchange process, governments minted coins, or made them by stamping them out of metal. They were minted in standard denominations, which made it easier to know the coins' values.

By taking on the responsibility of minting all coins, these ancient governments also took control of the economic well-being of their people. The gold coin stamped by Rome was not only worth its weight in gold, but it also was worth the power of the Roman Empire. It was possible for a citizen of Rome to use Roman coins to conduct business from the British Isles all the way back to Rome and beyond.

When these great empires collapsed, their coins remained valuable because they were made of rare metals. As a result, they were often melted down to be made into other currencies or for other uses. Still, gold and silver remained valuable long after the power of the empires had disappeared.

THE GOLD STANDARD

Understanding that gold has value and has been used as a currency across large geographic areas helps us understand why

The valuation of the yuan, the Chinese currency, has been a heated issue between the United States and China, as it directly relates to China's continuing role as a manufacturing nation.

people feel more comfortable with their wealth being in gold, rather than paper money. As people became more and more trusting of their governments and more assured that their governments would protect both their safety and their money, nations were able to introduce paper money.

In some parts of the world, the use of paper money was enforced by the government; in other places, the use of paper money evolved naturally over time. China is an interesting example because it began using nonprecious materials as currency as far back as 800 CE, during the Tang dynasty. The explorer Marco Polo wrote about the use of paper money during his travels through China. At that time, China's emperor was the only entity that could create paper money. Anyone could use paper money to exchange for gold at the central bank, but only the government could convert gold into currency. China also did not have many precious metals to make coins and invented the printing press (which further encouraged the use of paper money).

The reasons for government management of the gold supply have evolved over time. Initially, governments saw gold as a way to gain and keep power. During wars and other hard times, it was especially important for the rich and powerful to maintain

Many global monetary policy decision makers are outside the United States today. The growth of Asian nations has outpaced many others, and their influence on global affairs is tremendous.

control of as much wealth as possible. So even if a country's paper money became worthless (such as when a government printed a lot of money to pay for a war), the government would still have gold and be able to rebuild.

As governments evolved and took a more active role in the lives of their citizens, gold was used even more as a tool to keep the economy healthy and growing. But as governments evolved even further, the gold supply had difficulty keeping up with the amount of money in the world economy.

When more people work and create value in the economy, it creates an economic boom. The boom causes the price of goods to rise. To keep the increase of the price levels at a steady rate, the central bank adds money to the economy. This addition of new money to the economy helps keep inflation in check. Inflation is a natural part of the growth of the economy, and when it occurs at a low and stable rate, it can be good (low would be around 3 percent to 5 percent per year). Inflation can be bad when it happens too quickly (hyperinflation) or happens in reverse (deflation). Therefore, inflation is a force that must be managed. The gold standard system discouraged central banks from producing drastic increases in the money supply. This was supposed to help keep inflation under control.

CHAPTER THREE

HISTORY OF THE GOLD STANDARD

The gold standard's peak was from about 1883 to 1915. This period is viewed by some economists and historians as the golden age of growth due to a dramatic increase in the number of jobs available, in business activity, and in the growth of workers' wages and purchasing ability throughout the industrialized (highly developed) nations. Some economists feel that the use of the gold standard was the reason for the prolonged recovery following the Great Depression. Some argue that because the Federal Reserve kept interest rates high and the money supply low, the rebound took longer than it should have.

Historians look at what took place in the United States and the United Kingdom between 1816 and 1944. In 1816, the government of England passed the Gold Coinage Act, and by 1819, it had formally adopted a gold standard for the basis of its currency. Between 1819 and 1834, the United States had operated under a bimetallic system in which both silver and gold were the basis of the dollar. But in 1834, the United States adopted the gold standard. Gold was the standard until 1873, when the United States passed the Gold Coinage Act that excluded silver as currency, leaving gold as the only standard on which to base money. In 1900, the United States passed the Gold Standard Act, which formally adopted a gold standard for the U.S. dollar.

The year 1913 saw the passage of the Federal Reserve Act that established the Federal Reserve, an independent arm of the U.S. government. The Federal Reserve was made responsible for the maintenance of the U.S. money supply and the U.S. gold reserves. The outbreak of World War I, which lasted from 1914 to 1918, caused governments to break the gold standard conventions and issue more money than they had gold in order to back the effort to raise funds for the war. Because governments were printing more money than there was gold in their reserves, the United States halted the exportation of gold in 1917. The United Kingdom did the same in 1919.

The free movement of gold was reinstated in 1925, when the United States and the United Kingdom set a fixed gold exchange rate of $4.86 (£1). This would only last until 1931, when the United Kingdom suspended the gold standard. Then

World War II marked a new era in global economic power. American wealth and manufacturing enabled the Allies to defeat the Axis powers and fostered a new era of America's financial might.

in 1933, President Franklin D. Roosevelt passed the Emergency Banking Act, which required all Americans to surrender their gold for the new U.S. dollar, set at the exchange rate of $20.67 per ounce of gold. A year later, Roosevelt raised the price of gold to $35 per ounce.

The outbreak of World War II (1939–1945) forced countries to again abandon the gold standard in order to use inflationary practices to raise funds for the war. Following the end of the conflict in Europe, the United States convened the world powers to usher in the Bretton Woods agreement, which created both the World Bank and the International Monetary Fund (IMF) as instruments to help foster recovery around the world. The Bretton Woods system also established the U.S. dollar as the world's currency by linking the global price of gold to it. Foreign nations transacted their gold reserves in U.S. dollars, making it a very important currency.

GOLD RESERVES

The gold standard system has several components, including gold bullion, gold reserves, and exchange rates. Gold bullion is a bar of gold minted out of 99.999 percent pure gold. This is probably the purest gold that you can find anywhere, even more pure than the gold used in jewelry, which is around 97 percent gold. Gold bullion is forged, cast, and stamped by the country that owns it. Each country has its own bar standard of weight, dimension (length, width, and height), and marking. Anyone involved in the legitimate trading of gold can use this standard to identify where the gold came from, who owns it, and how much it is worth.

Inflation

Inflation is the natural increase in the price of goods and services that occurs due to economic growth. As more people purchase goods and services, the price levels tend to rise. With the rise in prices, the value of the currency—the money used to purchase goods and services—loses value. Inflation is kept within a healthy range by the activities of the central banks of the world. As the inflation level rises, central banks remove money from the system by raising the interest rate they charge to commercial banks to borrow money from the central bank. In response to the increased cost of borrowing money from the central banks, commercial banks raise the rates they charge borrowers. Those borrowers are usually businesses and individuals who use the money they borrow to purchase goods and services. Since they have to pay more to borrow money, they tend to borrow less and thus purchase less.

By using the available tools, the central bank is able to slow the growth of the economy just enough to lower inflation to a more desirable level. This is important because booms, or periods when everyone in the economy is on a spending spree, are dangerous: they create bubbles, or hazardous increases in price levels.

An example of the effect a bubble can have on the economy is the stock market correction of 2002. From 1997 through 2001, investors got caught in a frenzy of technology stock purchasing, hoping to get rich from the seemingly endless increase in stock prices of new Internet wonder companies like Yahoo! and AOL. In 2002, the prices of those tech stocks had gotten so out of control that the entire market collapsed, lowering the tech stock prices very quickly.

Gold bullion held in gold reserves was often needed by governments during the gold standard era. Bullion was pulled out of vaults and sold to other nations or on the market in order to raise cash. This was necessary because under the gold standard system, the central bank could not simply add more money to the economy. In order to put cash into the system, it had to sell its gold to other governments. The cash from these sales was then used by the government for whatever purposes necessary.

Governments set specific rates of exchange for their currency into gold. From this system, two countries could figure out how much their currencies were worth according to each government's standards. For instance, if country x has its rate of conversion from cash to gold at 5:1 and country y has its conversion from cash to gold set at 10:1, it is easy to see that the exchange rate from x to y = 5 to 10.

There were many steps taken to move gold from one country to another. Gold moving from the United States to the United Kingdom was inspected, weighed, and transported across the ocean. Sometimes, gold never actually moved from one country to another. Instead, it moved from one bank vault to another vault in the same city, even though the gold traded belonged to countries from across the globe. This system was built on trust and integrity. Governments trusted each other with their gold. There were auditors and inspectors from all countries who would verify that gold had been moved and that it was secure.

There are also costs to maintain gold. The first cost is an extraction cost, which is the cost of getting the gold out of the ground and refined. There are transportation costs for carrying

This vault in Switzerland is home to a large amount of the world's gold reserves and is one of the many specially designated safes belonging to foreign nations and investors.

large quantities of gold from a handful of mines around the world to the storage vaults. Creating and maintaining large and secure gold vaults also has costs. Once the gold has been transported to a safe vault, it has to be handled, measured, cast, stamped, and measured again. Then the gold is placed in the vaults, where it awaits trade or future smelting to a smaller size. Gold must be guarded by lots of well-trained, armed people, and the vaults must be kept in good condition. The carrying costs of gold bullion are very high.

Economist Roger Garrison estimates that the annual cost to carry gold bullion in today's U.S. economy would equal 2 percent to 3 percent of the U.S. gross domestic product (the total production of the economy) per year.

MYTHS and FACTS

MYTH Gold reserves are traded at the same price that gold in the commodity markets is traded.

FACT Gold reserves are traded at a fixed international price of U.S. $42.22 per troy ounce (a troy ounce is about 10 percent heavier than a standard ounce). Gold reserves are traded only between governments at this fixed price. Common gold that is traded in the commodity market is valued by the supply and demand in the market. As of this writing, gold is trading at U.S. $1,101 per troy ounce.

MYTH The gold that is used in international gold reserve bullion is the same gold that's used in making jewelry.

FACT Gold bars used for international reserves are 99.5 percent pure gold. Gold used for typical jewelry and private transactions is between 90 and 99 percent. This is measured using the karat system. Gold bars stored as international reserves each weigh approximately 27 pounds (12 kilograms), and modern minted bars are typically trapezoidal in shape. Each bar is stamped with information telling where the bar was created, what its purity is, and which country owns it.

MYTH In a gold standard system, everyone must at some point carry gold around in order to buy things.

FACT The fact is that under the gold standard system, anyone could go in and redeem paper money for a corresponding amount of gold. However, because gold is so easily stolen and quite heavy, it didn't make any sense for the average person or business to carry or hold any gold at all. Rather, all of the gold sat in bank vaults and people carried out transactions with paper money, just like we do today.

CHAPTER FOUR
MOVING FROM THE GOLD STANDARD

The most important thing to note about the history of the gold standard is the tendency of governments to drop the gold standard when they need to raise money. This reinforces how the gold standard keeps the growth of money stable. The two world wars were very expensive, and it would have been very difficult for nations to pay for them on the gold standard systems. So they simply abandoned the gold standard temporarily, printed more money, and issued lots of debt.

This is the next evolution of the money supply, the transition to the system of fiat money, or fiat currency. This transition was gradual, but the end of World War II was the real marker for the beginning of the change. The reason this transition was possible was the simultaneous need for massive amounts of cash for the rebuilding of the developed world and the arrival of complex financial systems. Governments and private banks were able to work together to raise enormous sums of money

Joseph Stalin was the leader of the United Soviet Socialist Republic (USSR). Following the end of World War II, the United States stood against the USSR to stem the spread of Communism to other parts of the world.

by selling bonds to the public. It was necessary for the government to raise more money than it was able to under the gold standard system; this was made possible by the borrowing of cash from individuals and other countries. In effect, the U.S. government was creating new money that was not linked to any gold at all.

Though this practice would have been rejected only thirty years earlier during the peak of the gold standard, the world was desperately in need of rebuilding. The United States exited World War II as the only real superpower that could be counted on to provide relief and defense from the growing threat of Communism to the east. When the need for rebuilding was combined with the threat of Communist Russia, it created a highly dangerous situation that made many feel that the hazard of maintaining a gold standard far outweighed the benefits.

In addition to the rebuilding effort and the Communist threat, the most fundamental factor that enabled the dramatic transformation away from the gold standard to a fiat system is the people's trust in government. People as a mass entity have ceded complete trust to their government because of the spread of democracy and representative government.

Fiat currency is a freely traded currency backed only by the good faith of the government. This good faith is the trust that people place in their government and their fellow citizens. We trust that the government will protect us and that our money has value because our government has our best interests in mind. This is possible because of laws, peace, and civility.

What Are Exchange Rates?

An exchange rate is how much of one currency it takes to equal a unit of another currency. For example, the exchange rate between the U.S. dollar and the Japanese unit of currency, the yen, could be U.S. $1 equals 90 yen. Exchange rates are used to figure out the price of goods and services from different countries. If a cell phone from Japan costs 4,500 yen, it also costs $50. The exchange rate between the United States and Japan changes all the time. But under the gold standard system, many countries linked their currencies' values to gold at fixed rates.

ABANDONING THE GOLD STANDARD

The end of the gold standard began with the close of World War II and the introduction of the Bretton Woods system. The transition from the gold standard to fiat currency in the United States happened over the course of twenty-seven years. In 1971, President Richard Nixon finally and officially put an end to the gold standard system in the country. What emerged was the dollar reserve system, a de facto use of the U.S. dollar as the replacement for gold in central banks around the world.

There are two key reasons why the world followed the United States in abandoning the gold standard. First, more flexibility was needed in setting the money supply. Second, the United States did not have the necessary gold reserves to meet the growth of the economy.

43

On August 15, 1971, President Richard Nixon cancelled the convertibility of the U.S. dollar to gold. This action effectively ushered the gold standard out of the modern U.S. financial system.

As discussed earlier, most countries have a central bank, which is responsible for the maintenance of the currency and setting interest rates for lending. These are the only tools that a central bank like the Federal Reserve has to keep the

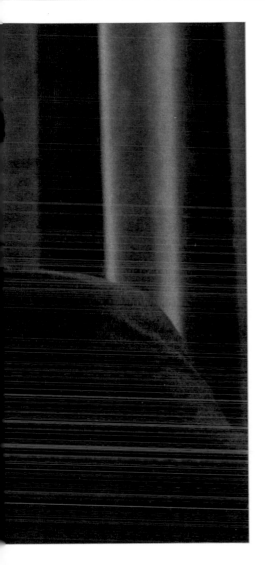

economy moving forward. Under the gold standard system, the supply of money is linked to the growth of gold in reserve and can only grow at the rate that new gold is added to the total supply. So in situations like wars, when governments need lots of money, the gold standard is a very inhibiting system. Abandoning the gold standard system allows governments to increase or decrease the money supply at will.

IMPACT OF ABANDONING THE GOLD STANDARD

The initial impact of the abandonment of the gold standard was in most ways contained to governments and major banks. The average citizen didn't have any real sense of the impact of the transition to a fiat system. A loaf of bread was still the same price it was the day before, along with most other goods and services. The most dramatic difference was that paper money was no longer exchangeable for gold. The real impact of the transition away from the gold standard was gradually felt by the average citizen, while it was immediately notice-able to bankers and governments.

However, between 1946 and 1971, there were several sub-stantial changes that occurred to inflation, employment, price levels, and domestic output. Inflation rose dramatically, but employment rates increased following the abandonment. The price and output levels of goods and services stabilized dramat-ically after abandonment. Overall, things generally improved when the fiat system was adopted.

The fiat system provides a dramatic improvement to the cen-tral banks' ability to manage the supply of money in the economy. With this system in place, and the rise of the modern bank-ing system, the world was poised to see the emergence of the golden age of debt financing under the fiat system.

CHAPTER FIVE
OTHER MONETARY SYSTEMS

The introduction of the fiat system heralded the beginning of a new era of finance and international banking. Though it cannot be said that the fiat system caused any of the major changes that occurred, its adoption was a small factor in the acceleration and adoption of many of these changes.

Though this book is dedicated to discussing the gold standard, one must take time to acknowledge the incredible impact that technology has had on trade. In order to understand just how profound the change was from how trade was conducted in 1900 to how it was carried out in 1946, all one needs to do is consider the technologies introduced in that period.

Radio became widespread, telephone lines were laid across the oceans, trains crossed entire continents, and airplanes could fly over the oceans in a single day. In 1900, it would have taken at least a week for a single message to move from New York to London, and another week for the reply to reach the sender. It would seem that the end of the gold standard may not simply have coincided with the technological revolution, but that these advances were positively impacted by the standard's end.

Each currency has an exchange rate with all other currencies. As money moves around the world each day, the value of currencies fluctuates.

GLOBAL CURRENCY MARKETS

In the new world of rapidly increasing international trade, new methods for exchanging currency were needed. The explosion of international transportation and trade caused the natural creation and evolution of a highly sophisticated system of global currency exchange. Not only did governments get better at managing exchange rates, but actual exchanges developed where people could trade large quantities of currency.

The rise of the currency markets was only possible when currencies were free to "float." Each country has its own currency, and that currency can be converted into other currencies. Each currency has its own value, which changes with the changes in the economy. Each currency's value is independent of other currencies and can be said to float on its own. This occurs only when the government allows its currency to float freely and does not interfere with its value.

Some countries "peg" their currency on other currencies.

This means they set the value of their currency to the set amount of another currency.

In the last ten years or so, the most public case of currency pegging was China pegging its yuan to the U.S. dollar.

The World Bank is an international financial institution that acts, as its name describes, as the world's bank. Among other things, it provides loans and capital to help nations develop.

This had the effect of keeping the value of China's currency artificially low—and keeping lots of new business flowing into China.

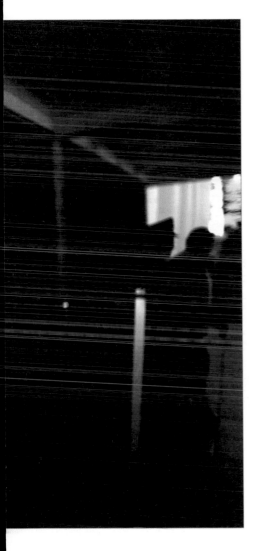

THE WORLD BANK

The World Bank was also created at the end of World War II during the Bretton Woods sessions. The primary charter of the World Bank is to make loans to countries with high levels of poverty. It makes money available with low interest rates to help developing countries support their people, businesses, and trade capabilities.

The World Bank is comprised of 186 member nations and is a self-governing, nongovernmental organization. It does not answer to any one nation. Rather, it serves all nations in need and determines its own course.

The World Bank does very important work to help eradicate poverty by making loans to poor nations and providing guidance and support for borrowers to help create lasting economic improvements.

51

The International Monetary Fund

The International Monetary Fund (IMF) is a multinational non-governmental agency funded and supported by nations around the world. It was created during the Bretton Woods sessions following the end of World War II. Its current charter is to provide general advice and analysis to its 186 member countries, along with providing loans to developing nations in need of assistance and to countries with high levels of poverty.

The IMF is similar to the United Nations in that it is not controlled by any individual government but is an independent entity with representatives from all of its member countries. Member countries are asked to support the IMF based on their relative economic prosperity, so rich countries pay more than poor ones.

THE FED AND U.S. MONETARY POLICY

The new ability the government had to exercise additional control of the U.S. money supply, coupled with its ability to set interest rates, made the U.S. Federal Reserve an extremely important part of the world economy. The Federal Reserve is responsible for creating and selling new U.S. bonds, notes, and bills. Bonds, notes, and bills are very similar. They are basically a promise that if you give the government some money today, you will receive a series of payments each year until you are paid back in full in the future. The lender gets the benefit of receiving more money than it loaned, and the borrower gets cash in hand. Because the U.S. economy was no longer

The U.S. Mint is responsible for the printing of currency and increasing circulation at the request of the Federal Reserve.

tied to a finite gold reserve, it became possible for the United States to dramatically increase the total supply of money in the economy. It is important to understand that the Federal Reserve doesn't simply print more money. It borrows money from other countries and private citizens, and in return, it must eventually pay back that money with interest. This is very important because if the federal government were to simply start printing new money, it would cause dramatic inflation, which would mean that all of the money in the hands of the public would lose value.

Because the Federal Reserve can quickly and easily bring lots of new money into the U.S. economy through debt sales, it becomes responsible for the health of the country's economy as well as the global economy. This makes the trustworthiness of the government critically important. If the government doesn't behave responsibly, it could harm both U.S. and world economies. Because of this, the country must pay very special attention to what the Federal Reserve and the U.S. government do with the dollar.

Ten Great Questions
to Ask a Financial Adviser

1. If I invest in gold, where does the gold go?

2. Should I invest in currencies?

3. Is there a safe way to invest my money so that it won't lose value?

4. How can I invest my money to protect it from inflation?

5. Can I buy foreign debt?

6. What is the difference between buying gold and gold futures?

7. What happens to my money if I invest in the debt of a foreign government that eventually collapses?

8. What is the difference between the gold you buy in jewelry and the gold you invest in?

9. Is it possible to invest in companies that mine for gold?

10. When is a good time to invest in gold?

CHAPTER SIX

UNDERSTANDING THE GOLD STANDARD TODAY

Using the example of a lemonade stand again, imagine that your neighbor comes up and wants a glass of lemonade but doesn't have any money. Then along comes another neighbor who agrees to lend money to the other neighbor for the glass of lemonade. Then the neighbor who loaned the money realizes that he needed the money for something else. Along comes a third neighbor who offers to give that neighbor some money. In exchange, he will collect the money owed to the second neighbor.

This may seem simple, but this is exactly what the practice of selling a loan is. Banks were buying and selling loans like mad throughout the early 2000s in an attempt to make money by passing the risk of the loan on to other parties while keeping a piece of the original profit. This is a very good example of using a tangible asset as the basis for a complex system of trade. Again, the only difference is that the asset in this case is not gold but a house.

Who Owns America's Debt?

As of this writing, the total outstanding U.S. public debt is approximately $12.44 trillion. The U.S. Congress has a statutory limit to the total debt that can be issued, set at $14.294 trillion, meaning that America has an additional $1.91 trillion it can issue before a new cap needs to be legislated.

The size of these numbers is staggering and somewhat hard to comprehend. If you consider the total size of the outstanding debt in light of the discussion of this book, it should be clear that under a gold standard system there is no possible way to have enough gold to represent $12.44 trillion.

As mentioned earlier, the Federal Reserve holds $190 billion of foreign gold in New York City, and the U.S. Treasury holds $145 billion of U.S. gold at Fort Knox. The combined total is only $335 billion, or about 2.69 percent of the total debt outstanding. National debt levels at this scale are possible because of the separation of the gold standard from the currency value.

THE 2008 HOME LOAN CRISIS

What is a mortgage? Mortgages are loans that banks make to allow people to purchase real estate. The bank gives the borrower money so that the person can make the purchase. In return, the borrower promises to pay back the loan over a period of time. In the event that the borrower fails to pay the loan, the bank has the right to repossess the property in order to reclaim its money.

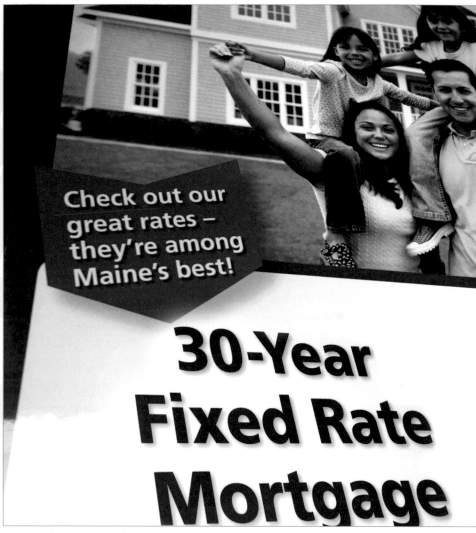

Check out our great rates – they're among Maine's best!

30-Year Fixed Rate Mortgage

The housing bubble in the early 2000s was fueled by the creation of complex loans. Today's financial crisis is blamed by some on the housing bubble.

In theory, this is a wonderful arrangement because both parties involved gain something of value. The bank gets paid back with interest, and the borrower gets to have his or her own home. This is a delicate relationship that can be affected by

either the bank or the borrower. Suppose the borrower loses his or her job, or suppose the bank goes out of business. What happens to the loan in either scenario? The delicate nature of loans requires that both the borrower and the lender keep informed of the status of each other in order to prevent anything bad from happening.

Just as gold was fixed in quantity in the gold standard, homes are also fixed in quantity for the most part. So when a bank makes loans for houses, it is investing in something that in theory could only grow at the same rate that it receives its interest payments. Since banks want to grow and can only grow when they make lots of investments, it makes sense to free some of the money loaned to borrowers by selling the loan to someone else.

Eventually, things got too exciting and many of the people involved in the housing bubble did things that were not very good for the rest of the group, and the whole system came crashing down. This same kind of situation happened in the days of the gold standard as well. In 1907, there was a terrible financial calamity in the United States that caused a major panic and a major stutter in the economy. It was eventually fixed with the passage of the 1913 Federal Reserve Act, which created new rules and systems to keep that from happening again.

THE PETRODOLLAR

The clearest example of a modern equivalent to a gold standard system is the use of the dollar in traded oil reserves. The standard currency used to trade oil around the world is the U.S. dollar, meaning that a barrel of oil in Mexico has the same value as a barrel of oil in Russia. This is the same as the gold standard.

This system is referred to as the petrodollar system. The reason this came into existence is that for many countries, the U.S. dollar is used as a reserve along with gold, and the United States is the world's largest consumer of oil. So it is safe to assume that the value of oil is great to America. Additionally, countries around the world also purchase and hold large quantities of oil, called reserves, for use by their military or in the event of a shortage. Again, this is exactly the same case as with the gold standard. Also, oil is traded freely on an open marketplace at a price determined by the supply and demand for oil at any given moment. This is where the petrodollar and the gold

Oil prices swung widely during the recession of the early 2000s due to overspeculation by investors and commodities traders about the future demand for oil and the growth of the economy.

standard are not the same. The gold reserves held by governments were traded between governments at fixed prices, and the gold that governments held in reserve were not traded on the open market.

The final and most crucial difference between the gold standard and the petrodollar is that people consume oil every day and there will be a day when it is all gone. Gold is never consumed—it is used in lots of ways, but it is never consumed like oil.

The Future of the Gold Standard

In reaction to our current recession and the growing federal deficit, there is renewed support for a return to the gold standard in the United States by some political parties and individuals. The argument is that the gold standard prevents the federal government from oversupplying debt. They claim that despite the potential negative attributes that a gold standard brings to the economy, preventing the government from overspending, therefore keeping deficits low, outweighs the downsides.

One highly recognizable supporter of the return to the gold standard is congressman Ron Paul, who ran for president in the 2009 election race. He believes that a return to the limitations of a gold standard would prevent runaway spending by the government and foster a new era of fiscal conservatism.

One of the most famous speeches in U.S. history is the "Cross of Gold" speech made by William Jennings Bryant on July 8, 1896. Bryant was attempting to secure a position as the Democratic candidate for president. In his speech, he advocated for the bimetallic standard in which both gold and silver were used as the basis for the dollar. He supported the interests

As a fiscal conservative, or someone who supports disciplined financial accountability in government, Congressman Ron Paul says a return to the gold standard would keep America financially prosperous and economically competitive.

of the people in the western part of the United States who, for the most part, borrowed money from banks and lenders on the East Coast. His message was meant to convey the importance of preserving the financial interests of farmers and businesses by adding inflationary support to the dollar through the adoption of the bimetallic standard. His impassioned speech secured his spot as the Democratic candidate for president.

We have now covered the gold standard system, the transition to the fiat system, and the adoption of modern equivalents to the gold standard. We will finish this discussion by looking at the newest chapter in monetary policy and international trade: the emergence of the World Bank, the IMF, and fair monetary policy.

A GLOBAL STANDARD

As discussed earlier, after World War II and the Bretton Woods agreement, the governments of the world agreed to create two major institutions to monitor and maintain the health of the world economic system. These two institutions are the World Bank and IMF. These institutions are independent of any country or nation. They look out for the interests of all countries' banking systems. These institutions are much like the United Nations: they are made up of employees

Members of the International Monetary Fund meet in Washington, D.C., on April 25, 2009, during the heat of the financial crisis.

from countries all over the world and are both directed by a charter to do what is best for all people in all countries.

The creation of the World Bank and IMF signaled an evolutionary point in our global systems. These institutions were chartered to act independently of any government and were granted the authority to act in ways that served the interests of humanity. This was in direct opposition to what would be in the best interests of most governments. It signalled that the government was looking out for the best interests of all people.

In addition to creating institutions to look out for the best interests of the world economy, standardized banking policies have begun to be adopted around the world. These standardizations came out of a series of agreements called the Basel Accords. The Basel Accords basically created rules and guidelines for banks to use to measure and manage the risks of their investments. The benefit of this is that if all banks the world over use the same standards, just as in a gold standard, it will become easier for all people to have safer investments in their banks. The goal of the Basel System is the same as the aim of the gold standard—to find a set of standards that all participants can agree upon and follow.

GLOSSARY

bond A contract between two parties in which one party borrows money from another for a rate of return and certain legal rights and protections in the event that the borrower is unable to repay the lender.

central bank A bank that is chartered by a government to be responsible for the management of monetary policy and money within that country.

debt An obligation in which one party owes another an amount of money.

deficit The name for the condition in which an economy is importing more goods and services than it is exporting. It can also be a negative amount of dollars on a balance sheet.

deflation The decrease of prices of goods or services within an economy.

economics The field of study that analyzes the production, distribution, and consumption of goods and services.

fiat currency A monetary system in which only paper money is used as the basis of financial transactions.

gold bullion Quantities of gold used for exchange between parties in a transaction.

gold futures A financial contract that two parties enter in which one party sells the other the right to purchase an amount of gold at a date in the future at a price determined today.

gold market The totality of all the markets and exchanges around the world that collectively, through supply and demand, determine the price of gold.

gold specie A gold coin or equivalent coinage used to conduct monetary transactions.

Great Depression A substantial and prolonged global economic recession that began in 1929 and ended in the late 1930s. The unemployment rate in the United States during this time reached 25 percent.

hyperinflation The increase of the price of goods or services by 50 percent or more per month.

inflation The increase of the price of goods or services within an economy.

interest rate The cost that a lender charges a borrower on a loan.

investment The transfer of capital from one party to another for use in an endeavor that will yield a return on the amount given.

lending The transfer of money from one party to another in exchange for a promise to repay the money with interest.

liquidity The ample availability of supply and demand for a particular good or service.

monetary policy The set of decisions made by the central bank of a government that impacts the supply of money into the economy and the overall cost of money within the economy.

recession A contraction of the growth rate of an economy.

speculation The purchase of a financial instrument, property, or commodity with the expectation that the price of the object purchased will increase.

surplus The name for the condition in which an economy is exporting more goods and services than it is importing. It can also mean a positive amount of dollars on a balance sheet.

trade balance The difference of the value of the imports and exports within an economy.

treasury bills Financial obligations sold by the U.S. government to the general public.

volatility The range of price change in a financial instrument or commodity.

FOR MORE INFORMATION

Bank of Canada
234 Wellington Street
Ottawa, ON K1A 0G9
Canada
(800) 303-1282
Web site: http://www.bankofcanada.ca
The Bank of Canada is the central bank of Canada. It is
responsible for setting the primary interest rate charged
to banks and controlling the supply of money, and thus
inflation, in the Canadian economy.

Bank of England
Threadneedle Street
London EC2R 8AH
England
Web site: http://www.bankofengland.co.uk
The Bank of England is the central bank of England. It is
responsible for the maintenance of the monetary supply
and the economic and financial stability of England.

Board of Governors of the Federal Reserve System
20th Street and Constitution Avenue NW
Washington, DC 20551

Web site: http://www.federalreserve.gov
The Federal Reserve provides the United States with a "safe,
    flexible and stable monetary and financial system." It
    is responsible for the monetary supply and interest rate
    policy of the United States. It is an independent entity
    and not part of the executive, legislative, or judicial
    branches of the U.S. government.

Federal Reserve Bank of New York
33 Liberty Street
New York, NY 10045
Web site: http://www.newyorkfed.org/index.html
The Federal Reserve Bank of New York is one of the twelve
    banks that make up the Federal Reserve banking sys-
    tem. The New York Federal Reserve Bank is the largest
    holder of gold reserves of any banking institution in the
    United States.

Royal Canadian Mint
320 Sussex Drive
Ottawa, ON K1A 0G8
Canada
Web site: http://www.mint.ca
The Royal Canadian Mint is responsible for the printing of
    currency in Canada.

U.S. Department of the Treasury
1500 Pennsylvania Avenue NW
Washington, DC 20220
Web site: http://www.ustreas.gov

The Department of the Treasury is a federal agency in the executive branch. The Treasury is the agency responsible for managing the finances of the U.S. government, collecting taxes, and protecting the financial interests of the people.

WEB SITES

Due to the changing nature of Internet links, Rosen Publishing has developed an online list of Web sites related to the subject of this book. This site is updated regularly. Please use this link to access the list:

http://www.rosenlinks.com/rwe/hgsw

FOR FURTHER READING

Bayoumi, Tamim, Barry Eichengreen, and Mark P. Taylor.
　　Modern Perspectives on the Gold Standard. Cambridge,
　　MA: Cambridge University Press, 2008.
Bernanke, Ben S., and Robert H. Frank. *Principles of
　　Economics.* New York, NY: McGraw-Hill, 2004.
Eichengreen, Barry. *Globalizing Capital: A History of the
　　International Monetary System.* Princeton, NJ: Princeton
　　University Press, 2008.
Flandreau, Marc. *The Glitter of Gold: France, Bimetallism,
　　and the Emergence of the International Gold Standard,
　　1848–1873.* Oxford, England: Oxford University
　　Press, 2004.
Friedman, Milton. *Capitalism and Freedom.* Chicago, IL:
　　University of Chicago Press, 1982.
Friedman, Thomas L. *The World is Flat.* New York, NY: Farrar,
　　Straus and Giroux, 2005.
Keynes, John Maynard. *The General Theory of Employment,
　　Interest and Money.* London, England: Palgrave
　　Macmillan, 1936.
Levitt, Steven D., and Stephen J. Dubner. *Freakonomics: A
　　Rogue Economist Explores the Hidden Side of Everything.*
　　New York, NY: William Morrow, 2005.
Lewis, Michael. *The Big Short: Inside the Doomsday Machine.*
　　New York, NY: W. W. Norton & Company, 2010.

Lewis, Nathan, with Addison Wiggin. *Gold: The Once and Future Money*. New York, NY: Wiley, 2007.

Metzler, Mark. *Lever of Empire: The International Gold Standard and the Crisis of Liberalism in Prewar Japan* (Twentieth Century Japan: The Emergence of a World Power). Los Angeles, CA: University of California Press, 2006.

Skousen, Mark. *The Making of Modern Economics: The Lives and Ideas of the Great Thinkers*. Armonk, NY: M. E. Sharpe, 2009.

Skousen, Mark, and M. E. Sharpe. *The Big Three in Economics: Adam Smith, Karl Marx, and John Maynard Keynes*. Armonk, NY: M. E. Sharpe, 2007.

Smith, Adam. *Inquiry into the Nature and Causes of the Wealth of Nations*. London, England: W. Strahan and T. Cadell, 1776.

BIBLIOGRAPHY

Axilrod, Stephen H. *Inside the Fed: Monetary Policy and Its Management, Martin Through Greenspan to Bernanke.* Boston, MA: MIT Press, 2009.

Baubeau, Patrice, and Anders Ogren. *Convergence and Divergence of National Financial Systems: Evidence from the Gold Standards, 1871–1971* (Financial History). London, England: Pickering & Chatto, Ltd., 2010.

Bresciani-Turroni, Costantino. *The Economics of Inflation— A Study of Currency Depreciation in Post War Germany.* New York, NY: Hesperides Press, 2008.

Burg, David F. *The Great Depression* (Eyewitness History Series). New York, NY: Facts on File, 2005.

Cribb, Joe. *Eyewitness Money.* New York, NY: DK Publishing, 2005.

Drobot, Eve. *Money, Money, Money: Where It Comes from, How to Save It, Spend It and Make It.* Toronto, ON. Maple Tree Press, Inc., 2004.

Harvey, John T. *Currencies, Capital Flows and Crises: A Post Keynesian Analysis of Exchange Rate Determination* (Routledge Advances in Heterodox Economics). New York, NY: Routledge, 2009.

Kemmerer, Edwin Walter. *Gold and the Gold Standard.* Auburn, AL: Ludwig Von Mises Institute, 2009.

Kummer, Patrica K. *Currency*. New York, NY: Franklin Watts, 2004.

Mankiw, Gregory. *Principles of Economics.* 4th ed. Chula Vista, CA: Southwestern College Publications, 2006.

McConnell, Campbell, Stanley Brue, and Sean Flynn. *Economics*. New York, NY: McGraw-Hill, 2008.

Mead, Walter Russel. *God and Gold: Britain, America, and the Making of the Modern World*. London, England: Vintage Books, 2008.

Skousen, Mark. *Economics of a Pure Gold Standard.* Irvington-on-Hudson, NY: Foundation for Economic Education, 2009.

Sowell, Thomas. *Economic Facts and Fallacies*. New York, NY: Basic Books, 2008.

INDEX

About the Author

Peter Ryan earned his BA at Villanova, his MBA at RPI, and has worked on Wall Street. He currently resides in Saratoga Springs, New York, with his incredible wife, Aubrey, who is his life mate and inspiration and is also an author of children's reference books. Aside from writing, Ryan runs a carpentry business and an IT consultancy.

Photo Credits

Cover (top) © www.istockphoto.com/Lilli Day; cover (bottom), pp. 1 (right), 6–7, 10–11, 48–49 Shutterstock; pp. 1 (left), 3, 4–5 © www.istockphoto.com/Dean Turner; pp. 9, 19, 31, 40, 47, 56, 60–61 Mario Tama/Getty Images; p. 13 The Granger Collection; pp. 16–17 FPG/Hulton Archive/Getty Images; pp. 20–21, 63 Alex Wong/Getty Images; pp. 24–25 © Erich Lessing/Art Resource, NY; pp. 26–27 STR/AFP/ Getty Images; pp. 28–29 Pool via Bloomberg/Getty Images; pp. 32–33 Albert Harlingue/Roger Viollet/Getty Images; pp. 37, 58–59, 64–65 © AP Images; pp. 41, 44–45 Keystone Images/Getty Images; pp. 50–51 Win McNamee/Getty Images; p. 53 Mark Wilson/Getty Images; pp. 67, 70, 73, 75, 77 © www.istockphoto.com/studiovision.

Editor: Nicholas Croce; Photo Researcher: Marty Levick